CLICK HERE!

GETTING PEOPLE TO **ACT**

HOW TO **A**TTRACT, **C**ONVERT AND **T**RANSFORM STRANGERS INTO CUSTOMERS

BY **DAN DROZ**

PART OF THE MARKETING FITNESS SERIES

GETTING PEOPLE TO **ACT**

HOW TO **A**TTRACT, **C**ONVERT AND **T**RANSFORM STRANGERS INTO CUSTOMERS

BY **DAN DROZ**

CLICK HERE!
GETTING PEOPLE TO **ACT**

By **Dan Droz**

International Standard Number:
Library of Congress Catalog Number:
Printed in the United States of America
First Printing: August 2014

Every effort has been made to make this book as complete and as accurate as possible, but no warranty of fitness is implied. The information is provided on an as-is basis. The authors and Marketing Fitness Press shall have neither liability nor responsibility to any person or entity with respect to any loss or damages arising from the information contained in this book or from the use of the programs, suggestions or recommendations that may accompany it.

TO CATHY

PREFACE

Every day, millions of small business owners, perhaps like you, wake up to face the challenges of getting and keeping customers. And, increasingly, you're hoping your website can help. But, more often than not, very few prospects show up. And when they do, even fewer call, buy or even leave a trace of their visit. It can be downright frustrating.

The reason isn't because the sites don't have lots of facts about what you do and how you can save customers time, money or worry. In fact, most sites do such a good job of explaining what they do that visitors often get all the information they need to decide you're not the right company, product or service for them. So much for facts.

The sad fact is, facts about what you do isn't the most important thing to attract strangers and convert them to visitors, prospects, customers and advocates for your business. In saying that facts aren't important, I'm not implying that you should not use facts nor should you misrepresent anything on your site. Just, that there's a lot more to getting people to take action than talking about all the facts of your business. This book illuminates some of those things–to get people to **ACT**.

CONTENTS

PREFACE   7

I. INTRODUCTION: ABOUT INTERNET MARKETING

II. ATTRACTING VISITORS

III. CONVERTING VISITORS TO FRIENDS

IV. TRANSFORMING

V. CONCLUSION

VI. APPENDIX: ONLINE BUSINESS MODELS

TURN PAGE

TO LEARN MORE

I. INTRODUCTION: ABOUT INTERNET MARKETING

George and Georgette just hung their shingle, the sign for their new consignment shop proclaiming to the world that they were now "in business". Theirs, like signs that have been hung in front of businesses for generations, was proudly posted to accomplish a simple goal: *to attract customers*. It was designed with care and put up with the conviction that by announcing their existence, passersby would see it, be impressed with their storefront, walk in the front door and once there, actually buy a dress, hat or necklace.

Except, this shingle can't be seen from the street. In fact, it can't be seen at all unless their customer of the future happens to have a computer, smart phone or tablet. Their shingle is their website, hidden from view until someone stumbles upon it.

And, unlike signs and front doors of yesteryear, there is not just another consignment shop on the next block. There are thousands of storefronts easily accessed by their future customers and millions of websites either already (or about to be) posted, hidden from public view until they are found. In addition, once someone has entered this virtual front door, there is no dress, hat or necklace to try on.

To make a sale, George and Georgette need to either entice someone to visit them or make their products sufficiently clear and compelling that someone would actually purchase a product without being able to hold it.

Suppose someone doesn't find something in their store during that visit. With their actual store, George and Georgette can strike up a conversation and maybe even start the beginning of a customer relationship.

In their virtual store, they might not even know when someone came in.

George and Georgette are not alone. Many business owners face the same challenges, trying to figure out how to attract customers, convert them to a sale and develop a relationship. And some businesses have figured it out. Whether through help from consultants, books and workshops or their own trial and error, they've learned and applied the principles and practices that make websites work for businesses, whether they are brick and mortar businesses or those operating strictly online.

This book outlines some of those principles and practices, garnered by helping hundreds of businesses tackle these issues and our own research in what it takes to leverage your website and social media. It sets forth a simple premise: that to succeed, online marketing (and, in fact all marketing) needs to prompt people to ACT at each stage of the marketing funnel. We mean this in two ways:

ACT as in a commitment on the part of a stranger, visitor, prospect or customer toward further engagement with your company, product or service.

ACT as an acronym for the three critical stages of marketing that apply, whether you are online, offline or both, which are:

- **Attracting;** creating a reason to take an action such as coming to your site or other content you provide.
- **Converting**; facilitating one or more actions on the part of the visitor or prospect that leads to a purchase, donation or email capture.
- **Transforming**; the ongoing relationship that leads to repeat business, referral and brand advocacy.

A. YOUR ROLE AS AN ONLINE MARKETER

Before the internet, there weren't many media moguls. To distribute content to a wide audience, you needed to own a content distribution channel like a TV, radio or publishing network which required a lot of infrastructure and...a lot of money. Media networks like TV used a very simple model. They developed content or programming that people wanted to watch or consume and once people were consuming it, they sold access to these audiences through advertising.

With the internet, everyone can be a media mogul. With very little infrastructre (and funds), *you* can develop content, attract your own audiences and decide whether you want to sell products, services or information directly or monetize your traffic the old fashioned way – by allowing other companies to pay for access to your audience through advertising.

But, because of the lower barrier to creating and distributing content, there's a lot more competition. When everyone is a media mogul, you've got to provide a lot of value for people to choose you over someone else.

Before the internet, George and Georgette had only to worry about the consignment shops in the same neighborhood. Now they've got to worry about competing consignment shops around the globe who are promoting their own unique products, including through the biggest consignment shop in the world – eBay. And according to the laws of supply and demand, when there's a large supply of consignment shops and the same basic demand, it's much harder to compete. When you're the only consignment shop available, what you've got is fine. You don't have to be the best shop or marketer in the land. But when you're competing with every shop in the world, you better have either the goods or marketing strategy to stand out.

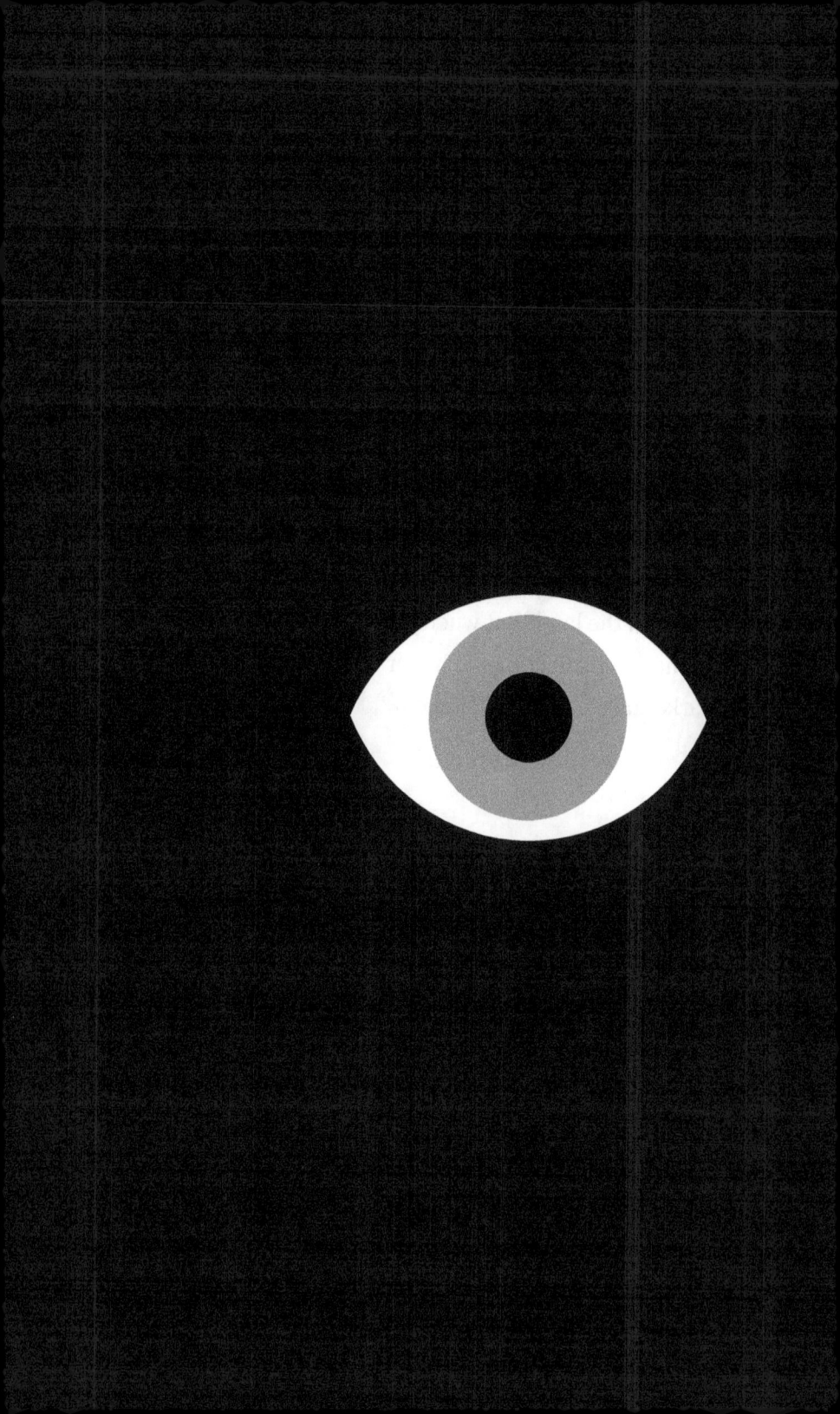

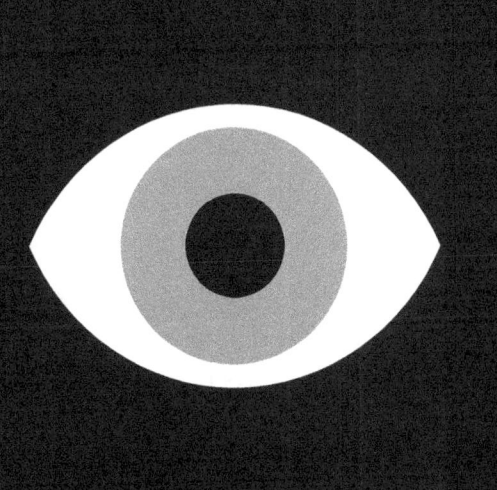

B. THE CULTURE OF THE INTERNET

Apart from more competition, there are several other important differences between internet and conventional business marketing, driven by both the nature of the internet and the culture it has spawned.

THE A.D.D. CULTURE. The first big difference is attention span. With so much information overload, people have changed the way and speed with which we consume information. Basically, our attention spans are shorter – we've got an attention deficiency! Even psychiatrists agree. Since 1997, a year before Google was founded, research has documented that the rate of Attention Deficit Disorder (A.D.D.), the name given by psychiatrists to describe a deficiency in our ability to concentrate for more than a few minutes, has increased an average of 3% per year from 1997 to 2003 and an average of approximately 5% per year from 2006 to 2011.

Whether this increase has been caused by the dramatic increase in information we're exposed to or something in our water, the effect is that people have a harder time concentrating on and absorbing information.

WE'RE A VISUAL CULTURE. Perhaps as a result of this overload, people aren't as willing to work very hard at digesting information. A picture has always been worth a thousand words, but now, a thousand words isn't even an option. There's just not enough time. If it's not easy to absorb, people just move on.

In addition, with the advent of mobile viewing, words are harder to read. Smaller screens make it harder to read a lot copy without a lot of work. It's not that we're lazier, although that could be argued. It just takes more effort to absorb content if there's a lot of it.

For example, the 140 character limit for tweets isn't arbitrary. The worldwide standard length of SMS (or text messages on phones) is 160 characters, so the founders of *Twitter* thought it wise to stay within those bounds.

140 characters was chosen as a good length, leaving 20 characters for the username of the sender. This way, anyone receiving a tweet via SMS would get the whole tweet in a single text message, with nothing spilling over into a second or third message that pops up minutes later. *Twitter* and other microblogging platforms as well are creating a new standard for messaging: short.

As a result, we've become, more than ever, a visual culture. Whether that means translating our messages into pictures, infographics or simply shorter chunks, the implication is that content, whether delivered through traditional media or the internet, needs to be thought of differently. More visually appealing or in much shorter chunks.

WHAT'S YOUR STORY? Together, the shorter attention spans and reduced appetite for long form content has increased the need to make our content more engaging and easier to digest. There are two ways to do this. One, as discussed earlier, is to visualize content through images and diagrams. The other is to simplify our messages by making them more like stories.

Stories have been around for a long time as a way to make information more digestible. The reason is that stories create associations through metaphor and narratives that help people frame the message as mental pictures. They also connect your message with universal themes that can make it easier for people to connect with your content.

Stories have important elements that people naturally connect to, the easiest of which is simply an 'example.' By using examples (or case studies), people can understand how your product or service can be applied to their own experience.

Another characteristic of stories is the plot, or sequence of events that provides a structure for content. Even the most sterile of services can often be broken down into a series of steps that makes a complex process easier to digest.

Underlying most good story plots are the three elements of a hero, a problem and a solution. The hero is the customer, the problem is the issue they're dealing with that you can address, and the the solution is your company, product or service. By framing your content in the form of a story where a reader or user can project themselves into the hero/problem/solution scenario, you can help them envision how you can solve their problem or satisfy their need.

One of the difficulties some businesses face is not clearly understanding or articulating their own story or process. How did you get started? What kinds of problems can you solve and what are the steps to using your product or service to solve that problem? Thinking about your own story can help make your content more engaging, memorable and persuasive.

COMMUNICATION
COMMERCE
COMMUNITY
CONTENT

C. TYPES OF SITES

There are four basic purposes of websites and the role your site plays will depend on the type of business you have and your own business goals. The strategies and tactics for leveraging your site will vary considerably, depending on the type of site you have, your business and how you are monetizing your website, sometimes referred to as the 'business model.' These four goals have been referred to as the 4 "Cs" and include:

COMMUNICATION, used primarily for brick and mortar (B&M) businesses where you are providing information or promotional messages about your business, products and or services without necessarily expecting an online transaction. Here, the goal is to convert a visitor to a prospect, where the visitors identify themselves and commit to contacting the company for additional information or purchase. Their target users go to them to find out more about a business. The sites don't specifically sell anything, but they do support sales by generating leads or making the user's buying decision easier. They are effectively 'brochure ware,' the equivalent of sales literature online.

For example, restaurant sites that post their menus, legal and accounting practices that post professional biographies, and practice descriptions and manufacturers that outline their capabilities, do not expect users to actually purchase these services online. They hope to prompt communication rather than transaction.

The internet began with these kind of sites because they are relatively inexpensive to produce and provide significant benefits. In many cases, a B&M company with products that can be represented and purchased online may also make it possible to allow users to make an online purchase.

COMMERCE, where products and services can be purchased on the website. Commerce sites can be used for both B&M businesses that have products and services that can be purchased online and businesses that sell exclusively online. Here, the purpose of the site is to convert a visitor to a customer, or in the case of non-profits, prompt donations or engagement with a cause. Non-profits use commerce sites not to purchase but to induce a prompt.

A classic commerce website like *Amazon.com* or *Buy.com* sells products, takes orders, charges credit cards, and ships goods.

Software and some information sites have the advantage of being able to deliver via internet download what they sell online, at the time of the transaction.

These sites normally offer their target customers the benefit of ease of use and selection. *Amazon.com*, for example, set the standard for commerce sites by offering a huge selection , offering a wealth of additional information on the products it sells and various ways to purchase.

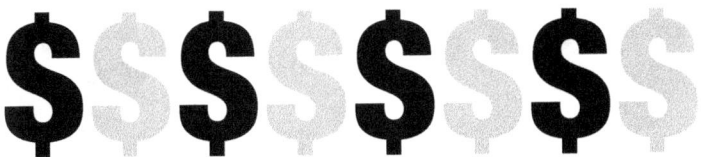

COMMUNITY, where the purpose is to create loyalty, membership or advocacy to a cause. Much like a bulletin board in a local super market, the business doesn't charge for posting notices on the board, nobody pays to read them, but the super market takes the trouble to manage the board because of the sense of community it brings to them, building traffic and loyalty. A typical community site offers email, bulletin boards and forums, a common focus for some group that has a common interest. Community sites are often started by groups, clubs or government organizations, but can also be sponsored by businesses that want to take advantage of a common interest. These might include a fan site sponsored by a sports team or sporting good stores to create brand loyalty.

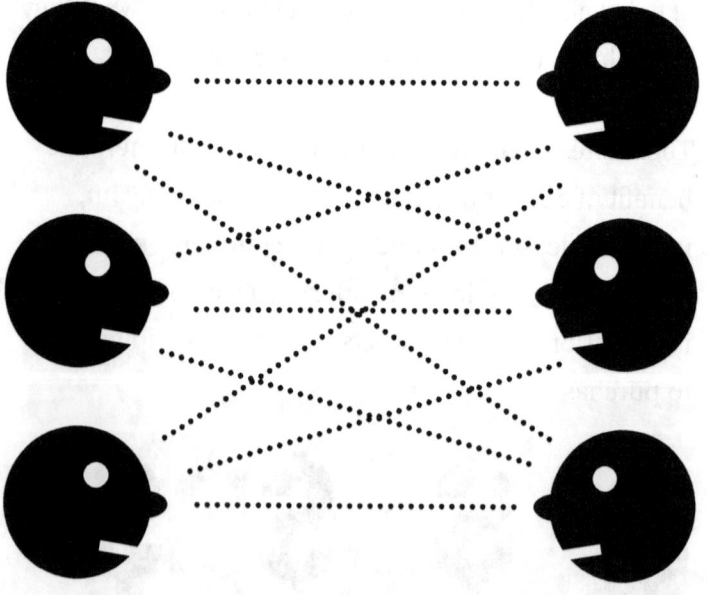

CONTENT, sometimes called 'publishing,' where the website is actually a medium that showcases valuable content that can be informative, entertaining, educational or persuasive. Although all sites have content which falls into these categories, a wholly content driven site monetizes traffic through advertising, much like traditional media such as broadcast and print publications provide content that attracts readers or viewers that provides an audience that advertisers pay to access. Users consume the product (news, as an example) at no charge and the site makes money by charging advertisers or sponsors for banner advertising or through affiliate purchase programs where users are prompted to make a purchase for another company's products or services where revenue can be shared. These are content sites that depend on Internet advertising or affiliates for their revenue.

The main point is that there should be a payoff for your business. Each form of website is designed for goals that align with your business and the "Cs" can be combined to enhance the effectiveness of your site.

ABC123

STRANGER VISITOR PROSPECT CUSTOMER

D. GOALS AND METHODS

Whether you have a 'bricks-and-mortar' or online business, the primary goal of marketing and the methods for achieving that goal are the same.

GOALS

The goal of all online marketing is to prompt strangers and visitors to commit to take **ACTions** that lead to *conversions* that can take the form of clicks on ads, contact with your company, memberships, engagement or transactions. *Transactions* may be defined as a purchase, donation, registration or other tangible commitment to your offering.

For websites, this goal can be rephrased as:
- Prompting **ACTions**
- on the part of **STRANGERS**
- to become **VISITORS** you are trying to convert
- to either **PROSPECTS** or
- **CUSTOMERS, DONORS OR BRAND ADVOCATES**,

where
- **STRANGERS** and **VISITORS** are anonymous,
- a **PROSPECT** has identified themselves
- and a **CUSTOMER, DONOR OR BRAND ADVOCATE** has committed to a transaction or other desired result.

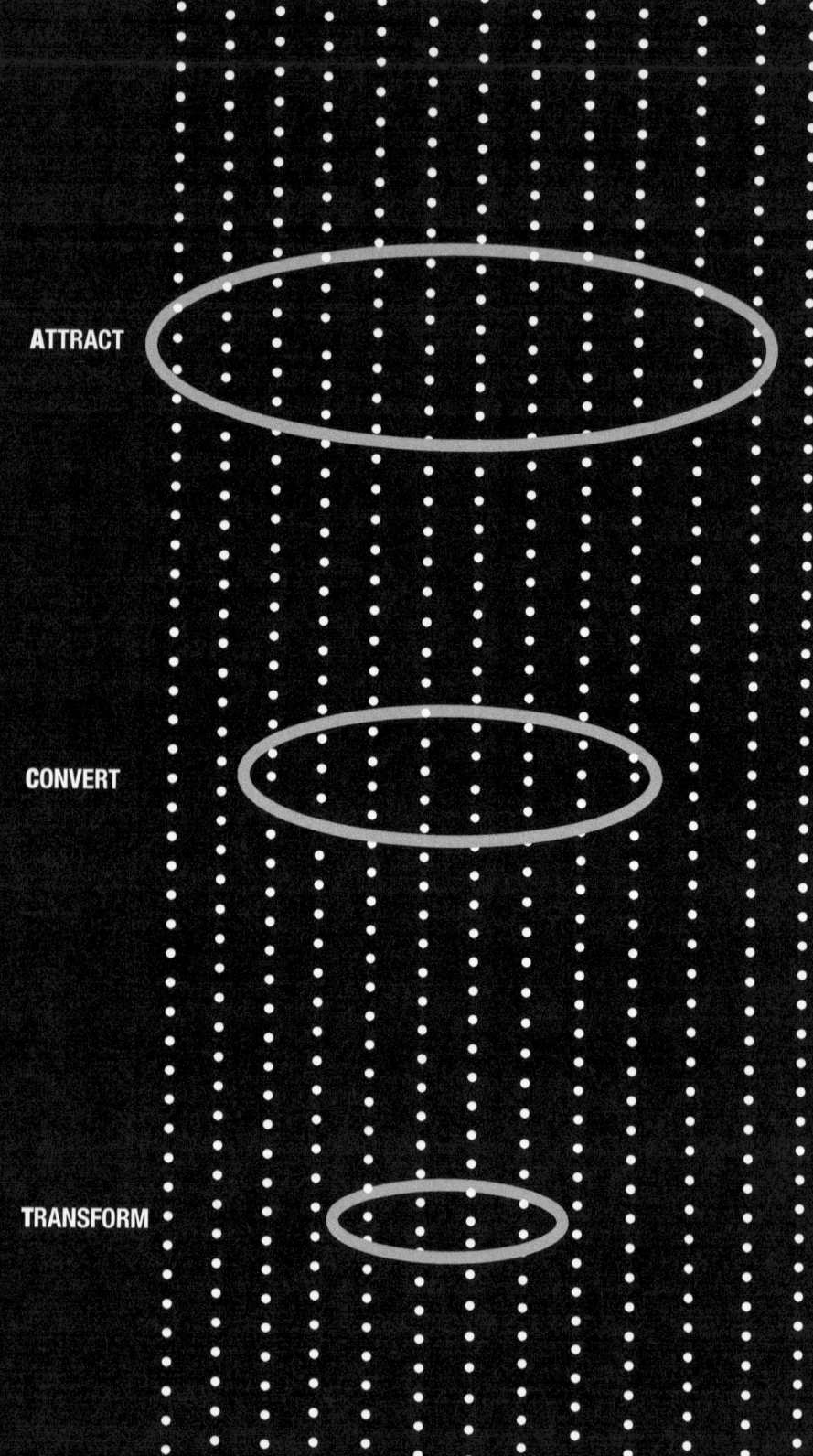

ATTRACT

CONVERT

TRANSFORM

There are three stages of **ACTion** to creating a relationship with a customer to engage them and prompt commitment.

ATTRACTING

Before you can influence visitors to your website, you've got to get them there. This involves targeting them, engaging them and prompting them to take the action of coming to your site.

CONVERTING

Once they've come to your site, you need to prompt them to take one or more **ACTions** that can lead to identifying themselves, further contact or purchase.

TRANSFORMING

Whether or not a visitor/prospect chooses to have further contact or make a purchase, you would like to have some 'bread crumbs,' including some information about their needs/interests and an email address that will enable you to continue your contact with them. If they leave your site without a trace, you have no way of influencing them.

II. ATTRACTING VISITORS

Before George and Georgette can influence any stranger to take action toward being a visitor, they need to, by definition, to get the stranger to their site. The same applies to you. The methods used will vary depending on the type of business and whether or not you know who your future customer might be. For example, if you sell products to nuclear power plants, there are only 64 such plants in the United States. In this case, you can and should contact and influence each of these prospects "directly." On the other hand, if you're a personal injury lawyer you can't know who is going to have an accident on any particular day. Whatever your site type or marketing strategy, the methods for **ATTRACTING** prospects include:

MEGAPHONES, outbound communication which prompts someone to visit your site. Here, promotional messages are entirely acceptable, even expected.

MAGNETS or SEO, where you attract visitors to your site through the relevance of your site's content to a prospect's online search.

MEET-UPS or Social Media, where online social relationships lead to deeper engagement and outright promotion is risky.

A. ATTRACTING BY MEGAPHONE

Particularly for businesses that do not know specifically who their customers will be, the first strategy is to create awareness of your business, product or service through broadcast advertising and/or promotion. This promotion can take place in both traditional and online media that include traditional broadcast and PR and online advertising and PR.

Traditional Broadcast

Even if your business is strictly online, traditional media such as TV, radio, print, outdoor, networking events, trade shows and public relations (editorial placement) can play an important role in creating awareness and "mindshare" of your business and prompt people to visit your site. This can be in the form of advertising, public relations, direct marketing and personal relationships. This is sometimes called "interruptive" marketing, because it is designed to attract attention away from the primary reason for viewing content. In traditional broadcast, print and outdoor media, there are four important concepts that impact the cost of your promotion: frequency, reach, audience, impact and position.

- **Frequency** is the number of times your ad or message is placed or 'run.' For example, you can run an ad once a month or once a week.

For many businesses, traditional media is necessary because they are trying to create general awareness of their products and services in specific locations or industries. For example, companies that operate in a narrow field such as the power plants market (top), there are very few potential customers, so advertising in trade publications or through direct marketing is an economical way to reach prospects. Some businesses need to keep their names in the public eye. This would apply to retail businesses such as car agencies and retail stores or personal injury lawyers (below). In these instances, onventional trade or consumer advertising that creates ongoing mind share is often an important part of driving traffic to their sites.

- **Reach** is the number of people (or impressions) your message reaches with each placement. If a publication reaches 100,000 people, it will cost considerably more than if only 50,000 people will view it.
- **Audience** is the profile of the viewers or readers you are trying to reach. Some audiences (such as high net worth individuals) are more valuable, so they often cost more to reach.
- **Impact** refers to the size or ad (if print or outdoor) or the length of the message (if TV or radio). In print, you can have a full page, half page or smaller. In broadcast, you can have 15 seconds, 30 seconds or longer.
- **Position** is the location or time slot where your message appears. You can have your ad on the back cover or within a publication. In TV or radio, you can choose certain "time slots."

You need to be very careful when choosing each, as you don't want to pay for impressions that are not relevant to your product or service. Important in any of these forms is a clear "Call to Action," a prompt for a reader, listener or viewer to **ACT** (visit your website) with an easy-to-find and memorable URL, QR Code or other Scan Code to your website. This prompt can also take the form of an 'offer' which increases the benefit of the action.

THE ALPHABET SOUP OF ONLINE ADVERTISING

Apart from traditional (off line) media, online advertising and promotion has become a cornerstone of outbound promotion for many businesses. There are three basic models for promoting your product or service online: Pay Per Impression (PPI), Pay Per Click (PPC) and Pay Per Action (PPA)

Pay Per Impression (PPI), or sometimes called CPM or "Cost Per Thousand (M)" is where you pay to have people view your ad or offer, whether or not they respond or interact. These ads are usually in the form of pop-ups or banners that appear adjacent to or over content on a site. and can be purchased through agencies, media buyers or often directly from a content provider. These can be very effective when placed on news sites or others where there is a large number of visitors each day.

Banner ads or "pop up" ads that appear on websites are forms of paid advertising or "interruptive" advertising. Just like with traditional broadcast, you can choose the frequency, reach, audience, impact and position.

Pay Per Click (PPC), where you pay only when someone clicks on your ad or offer. The principal form of online advertising is the 'Sponsored Link,' a headline/ad that you pay to present to someone using a a search term or target audience profile that you are trying to reach such as those sold and delivered through Google, Bing and Facebook. Your link/headline can appear as part of, or adjacent to, a search or can be presented to the visitor of another site. The value and price of each click is decided upon through an auction based on the search terms and the ranking you choose. In these cases, three issues are important:

Headline. Effective PPC, like all advertising, is driven by maximizing interest with a short but compelling headline that provides a reason for an interested searcher to click on your ad NOW. Below are three ads which demonstrate what a few words can do. You can monitor various ads you create and actually view which ones are receiving more clicks.

Left handed golf clubs Thomas Golf Irons Woods Hybrids with patented alignment features thomasgolf.com	Bad
Left Handed Golf Clubs - Guaranteed Low Price on **Golf Clubs** Free Shipping on Orders Over $75! ⌄ ⌄ Checkout 🛒 ➕ Show products from Golfsmith for left handed golf clubs www.golfsmith.com/Clubs	Good
Lefty **Golf** Sets for Less - Discount **golf** sets from just $119.9 Factory direct **left hand golf clubs** ⌄ ⌄ Checkout 🛒 www.golfandsports.com/lefty-golf	Excellent

Exclusions. In PPC, you pay for every 'click,' so your goal is not to maximize total clicks but to exclude any search terms that do not apply to your business. For example, if your business is *residential* real estate, you may want to exclude searches for *commercial* real estate to avoid having to pay for unwanted clicks.

Landing Pages. The PPC will go directly to a landing page on your site. The purpose of a landing page is to prompt **ACTion**. This page needs to be directly relevant to your PPC ad, specifically geared to the offer or search terms, audience or other qualifier. Landing pages can be an interior web page or a page that resides on your site, but is specifically tied to the PPC ad with a prompt for capturing emails or other directed 'ask.'

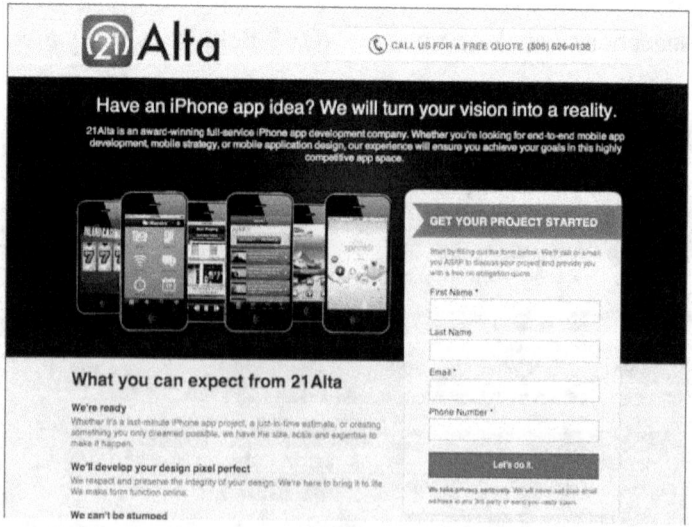

In this landing page, the call to action is a direct request for a person's contact information.

Pay Per Action (PPA), an affiliate model, where you are charged only after a specific **action is completed** such as a registration or transaction. For example, when you visit a site and see advertising for products offered through Amazon, and you purchase it, a percentage of that purchase goes to the site where it was posted. That site has agreed to place *Amazon* ads on it's site because they want to monetize their traffic by receiving a portion of the revenue that is paid by the purchaser.

There are hundreds of affiliate platforms that you can join and you only pay when someone actually purchases, registers or takes other 'action' you specify. In these cases, the content provider chooses what products and services to promote on their site, so your advertising proposition is important to being seen by prospects. This proposition can be a flat fee or revenue sharing as a percentage of the selling price. PPA can be very effective if you have a high value product or service or where a subscription/continuity program is involved.

In this affiliate PPA ad, the advertiser is not obligated to pay unless a particular "Action" is taken such as the purchase of the program that is advertised.

ASKO, Inc. Acquires Wapakoneta Machine Company

ASKO, Inc. Acquires Wapakoneta Machine Company

PR Newswire

HOMESTEAD, Pa., Jan. 13

HOMESTEAD, Pa., Jan. 13 /PRNewswire/ -- ASKO, Inc. a worldwide manufa
shear knives and wear parts for metal producers, processers, and recy
has recently acquired assets of The Wapakoneta Machine Company, expar
ASKO's already extensive product and service capabilities.

In acquiring Wapak intellectual property, machinery, equipment and
inventories, ASKO recognizes opportunities to serve new customers, e>
business and create growth. The integration of the Wapak business ir
will benefit ASKO customers, ASKO employees and strengthen the compar

Bill Rackoff, CEO of ASKO, remarked that, "ASKO's acquisition afford
Wapakoneta customers the continuous availability of tooling grades ar
outstanding performance they have long relied upon. ASKO's entire te
forward to servicing Wapakoneta customer tooling requirements."

CLICK HERE! Getting People to ACT

Online PR

Another method of online megaphoning is PR. There are a number of content distribution services such as *PR Newswire,* that, for a fee, will distribute your editorial content to news and editorial media that can provide good exposure. The internet has also spawned a large market for independent editorial content providers, where affinity groups are drawn to sites that have editorial content that may include reviews, or other information about a specific subject.

In the example on the facing page, a press release was prepared and submitted to *PR Newswire* that has relationships with thousands of media outlets that you can specify, some of which have millions of viewers. By distributing through such a service, your press release can automatically be posted in such places as *Bloomberg, Forbes* and trade publications that are relevant to your business.

Does anyone read these releases? Maybe. But even if no one reads them when they are posted, the content becomes accessible through search engines, creating backlinks to your site. Apart from backlinks, having your product or service mentioned in these articles can provide ongoing exposure and credibility and content which can improve your SEO, discussed on the following pages.

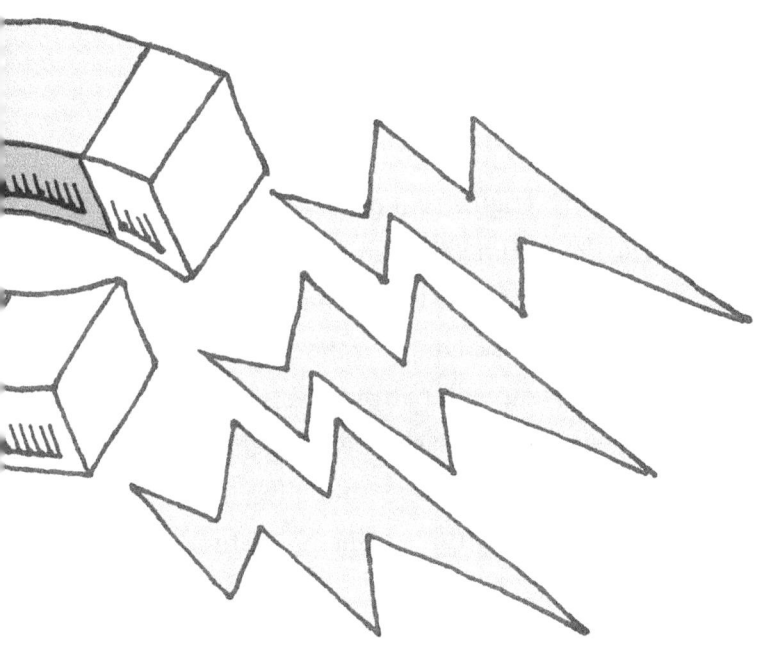

B. MAGNETIC MARKETING (SEO)

Apart from the broadcast forms of creating awareness for your company, product or service, there are also ways that you can attract visitors without paying for placement in either search engines or websites. These are referred to as 'organic' rather than 'sponsored' links, and come as a result of people finding your landing page or website through a search.

Search Engine Optimization (SEO) is a strategy for creating high search engine ranking as a result of understanding the parameters that make your site relevant to the term or terms that someone is searching for. When someone is searching for the type of product you offer, you want your company to be displayed as high as possible in the search engine being used (i.e., *Google*, *Bing*). The relevance and ultimate value of your site is determined by three principle factors.

CONTENT, CONTENT AND CONTENT

The first and most important feature of a site that makes it valuable is the content itself. Getting to the top is not about trying to trick the search engines. The engines are constantly tweaking their formulas, so today's trick won't work tomorrow anyway. And trying to stay on top of the tricks takes more time than simply making your site worthy of a good ranking in the first place.

Here are some suggestions for content:

Bricks and Mortar Businesses. If you have a bricks and mortar business, this amounts to being clear and informative about your offerings and creating a variety of page content that is interesting and compelling.

Stores/Commerce Sites. If you're running a store, think about what would make your store outstanding: Low prices or super-high-quality products (depending on the audience you're targeting), large selection, friendly, responsive customer service, easy ordering process, lots of information about the products you sell, customer reviews of the products.

E-zines. Try to create two new articles every week. If you can't do that, try to do one page each week. At a bare minimum, create a new article each month. As much as possible, your new articles should be unique, interesting, authoritative, and compelling.

Most importantly, purge your mind of trying to think of ways you can "trick" your way to the top of the results. Instead, build good, quality pages for your visitors, and trust that the rankings will follow.

MARKERS: KEY WORDS, METATAGS AND PAGE TITLES

The second important issues for SEO are the markers, the flags that search engines look for to indicate whether your content is relevant to a search term(s).

Key Words. Choose key words carefully. If you own an online golf supply store, do you make more sales from visitors searching for "golf clubs" or "golf balls?" Although keyword search tools such as *Google* analytics allow us to find the search terms people use, those tools cannot show us directly how valuable it is to receive traffic from those searches. There is no magic formula for understanding the value of a keyword. You need to understand your own website, make some hypotheses, test, and repeat. Here are some issues to consider:

Relevancy. Is the keyword relevant to your website's content and will searchers be happy with what they find on your site when they search using these keywords?

Placement. Are there search advertisements running along the top and right-hand side of the organic results? Typically, many search ads means a high value keyword, and multiple search ads above the organic results often means a highly lucrative and directly conversion-prone keyword.

Sample Campaigns. Buy a sample campaign for a keyword at *Google AdWords* and/or *Bing Adcenter*.

Test Traffic. If your website doesn't rank for the keyword, you can nonetheless buy "test" traffic to see how well it converts. In *Google Adwords*, choose "exact match" and point the traffic to the relevant page on your website. Track impressions and conversion rate over the course of at least 2-300 clicks.

Estimating the Value of Key Words. Using the data you've collected, you can determine the exact value of each keyword. For example, if your search ad generated 5,000 impressions, of which 100 visitors have come to your site and 3 have converted for total profit (not revenue!) of $300, then a single visitor for that keyword is worth $3 to your business. Those 5,000 impressions in 24 hours could generate a click-through rate of between 18-36% with a #1 ranking, which would mean 900-1800 visits per day, at $3 each, or between $1-2 million per year. Search Engine Optimization involves constant testing, experimenting and improvement. Remember, even though SEO is typically one of the highest return marketing investments, measuring success is still critical to the process.

Longtails. Going back to our online golf store example, it would be great to rank #1 for the keyword "golf clubs" - or would it? It's wonderful to deal with keywords that have 5,000 searches a day, or even 500 searches a day, but in reality, these "popular" search terms actually make up less than 30% of the searches performed on the web. The remaining 70% lie in what's called the "long tail" of search. The long tail contains hundreds of millions of unique searches that might be conducted a few times in any given day, but, when taken together, they comprise the majority of the world's demand for information through search engines.

Another lesson search marketers have learned is that long tail keywords often convert better, because they catch people later in the buying/conversion cycle. A person searching for "golf clubs" is probably browsing, and not ready to buy. On the other hand, someone searching for "best price on Callaway Apex Irons" practically has their wallet out!

Titles. Page titles signal that your site has rich content in a subject area and, when aligned with search terms, can attract visitors to that page. Write a <TITLE></TITLE> tag for each page that accurately describes that page (no more than about 64 characters).

BACKLINKS, PORTALS AND POPULARITY

An important criteria for attracting visitors is 'popularity:' how many people see your content as valuable. Popularity in the online world is largely determined by how many other sites have "backlinks" to your site, i.e., sites that "refer'" or link to your content. There are a number of ways to create these types of backlinks.

Portals and Directories. You can leverage the SEO of portals and directories that focus on your industry. For example, in the design and marketing field, there are a variety of "Creative Directories" that list firms and allow them to provide a description of their capabilities. Because of the focused content of these portals, they generally have high search rankings.

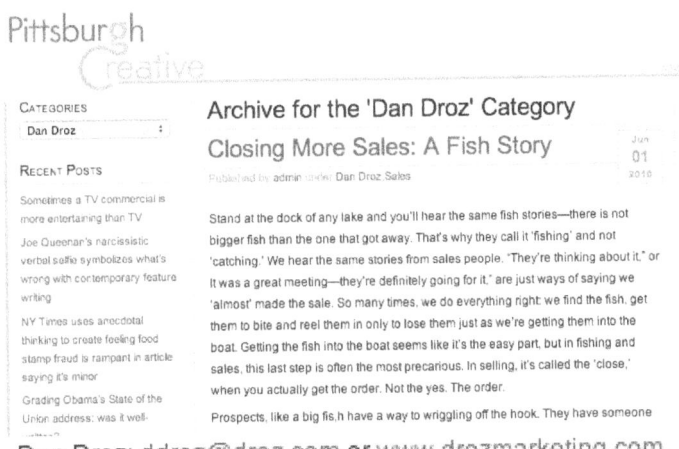

In this directory, blogs are used to provide content of interest to businesses, where the writer can provide one or more links to landing or specific site pages that are relevant to the content of the blog, providing both an incentive to visit the site and backlinks which improve SEO.

How do you make services tangible?

▶ ◀)) 0:02 / 3:56 ① CC ⚙ ▭ [ ]

Small Business Marketing Ideas Dan Droz- Selling Services

Dan Droz · 13 videos

▶ Subscribe 70

3,358 views

👍 17 👎 1

Dan Droz @DanDroz · Jan 10

DROZ Sweeps "Marketer of the Year" Awards... Again! #constantcontact conta.cc/1gV24RL

↩ ♺ 1 ★ 🔖 •••

Dan Droz @DanDroz · Oct 1

Tea Party @SenToomey embarrassed us by shutting down the government. Don't hold our country and our economy hostage any longer. via @padems

↩ ♺ ★ 🔖 •••

Dan Droz @DanDroz · Sep 5

The Future of Pittsburgh and the Bloomfield Brand #constantcontact conta.cc/1a9Exck

CLICK HERE! Getting People to ACT

Blogs and Review Sites. There are literally hundreds of sites that are looking for content like articles you can write that showcase your expertise or industry knowledge. These articles can reference other information that links those articles back to your site.

My favorite form of blogging is "Video Blogging," where I might just sit down and record short and informative videos that can be easily viewed and digested. These are posted on YouTube and get lots of comments and backlinks, all of which are linked to my website.

Just Ask. Don't forget to ask your vendors, customers and friends if they can provide a link back to your site from theirs.

SYNDICATION/RSS

Suppose you've written an article and want to distribute it to a number of outlets that will create backlinks to your site, or you simply want more people to see it. You can set up an RSS (Really Simple Syndication, AKA Rich Site Summary; RDF Site Summary) feed/channel which will automatically distribute your content to other outlets which can include blogs or social media outlets like *Twitter* and *Facebook*. In the example (left), we published on our *Facebook* page and it was automatically 'fed' via RSS, as a *Twitter* post.

C. MEET-UPS: ATTRACTION BY SOCIAL MEDIA

Where Megaphone and Magnet Marketing are understood to be promotional, social media is based on the value of community, so your authenticity and an understanding of the differences between various social media platforms is the critical element for success. Using social media for marketing may involve some of the same techniques as you would use to attract those to your website, but the potential for sharing is much greater. Metaphorically speaking, you should treat social media as though you were meeting people at a networking event or social occasion rather than at a trade show. At a trade show, it's expected to be 'selling.' At the reception following a trade show, it's about socializing and outright 'selling' is considered a bit of an overreach and may do more harm than good.

Although many platforms do not require linking to your website to have an effect, Social Media Marketing (SMM) employs various forms of social media networks to achieve marketing and branding goals through a culture rather than strictly through content. SMM primarily covers activities involving social sharing of content, videos, and images and, when your URL (either home page or landing page) is embedded into your messaging, can act both as a prompt to visit your site and and valuable backlink that enhances SEO.

THE CULTURE OF SOCIAL MEDIA

Many would like to think that social media is a homogeneous collection of people interacting and that all we have to do is provide really good comments, likes or photos and we'll be embraced by the whole world. But the ease with which we can enter conversations and submit content to the masses has created a much more nuanced environment. It's not just what we say or do, but *how*.

This, or course, has always applied to developing relationships, but online communications, for all its strengths and capabilities, has many limits. Like time, eye contact and not being able to retrench if you've made some sort of social faux pas.

Just as you express yourself differently at a dinner party than in a business meeting, so, the way we present ourselves in *Facebook* or *Pinterest* will be much different than *LinkedIn* or at an extreme, *Tumbler*. If you're not cool, don't even bother showing up at *Tumbler*, *Instagram* or *Vine*.

Also, each social media platform has it's own medium-specific way of dealing with content. Some are great for text and others rely on really good images.

CONTEXT, CONTEXT AND CONTEXT

What this comes down to is that social media platforms are more about *context* than content. Different social media platforms have different cultures and understanding these cultures is critical to leveraging them as a memes to drive traffic to your site. In traditional media such as broadcast TV, there are lots of different types of programming geared to specific audiences. Embedded in these differences is the aspect of context. But, it's all the same medium – TV.

The most important thing that distinguishes SMM from either Megaphone or Magnetic marketing is the additional emphasis on *context* as compared to *content*. For example, *Facebook*, has the broadest spectrum of users and operates much like your network of friends. You have a good deal more leeway in both the types of content and way you frame it.

CLICK HERE! Getting People to ACT

OVERVIEW OF SOCIAL MEDIA

There are a variety of social media platforms, including:

SOCIAL NETWORKS like *Facebook* and *LinkedIn* allow you to connect to others of similar interests and background. and usually consist of a profile, ways to interact with others and setup groups.

BOOKMARKING SITES like *Delicious* and *StumbleUpon* let you save and manage links to various websites and resources "tag" favorites for search and sharing.

SOCIAL NEWS like *Digg* and *Reddit* let you post news items or links to articles and "vote" on items. Those that get the most votes are displayed the most prominently.

MEDIA SHARING like *YouTube*, *Flickr* and *Instagram* allow you to upload and share media such as pictures and video and most have features such as profiles, commenting, etc.

MICROBLOGGING like *Twitter* focus on short updates that are pushed out to anyone who subscribes.

BLOG COMMENTS AND FORUMS of which there many, allow members to hold conversations by posting messages. Blog comments are similar except they are attached to blogs and usually the discussion centers around the topic of the blog post.

REVIEW OF SPECIFIC SOCIAL MEDIA OUTLETS

Here are some of the most popular social media outlets and some suggestions for leveraging them to create awareness and attracting them to content on your website.

Some things to keep in mind for all social media platforms. First, think mobile. Social media is not a place to get work done and most people on social media are interacting when they're supposed to be doing something else. Keep it simple. Second, although you can sell on most social media, making an 'ask' usually has to be buffered by giving of a lot of authentic, valuable content before you earn the social capital to ask. Third, spend some time on a social medium before you start to use it so you get a sense of the culture. Here are some of the most popular and valuable platforms to try out.

FACEBOOK is a casual, friendly environment and begins with creating a *Facebook* Business Fan Page. Pay careful attention to layout, as the visual component is a key aspect of the *Facebook* experience.

For businesses, a few things really matter in *Facebook*. *Facebook* is basically a photo gallery so pictures really matter. If it's a product, event or business related image, be sure to embed your logo into the photo and if there are people in photos, tag them. To prompt response, try asking a question. What do you think? How do you know you've been successful in *Facebook*? You can track your engagement numbers, likes, comments and shares. The more you get, the better you're doing.

GOOGLE+ is a *Facebook* competitor where you can upload and share photos, videos, links, and segment your followers into smaller groups, enabling you to share information with some followers while barring others. Also host video conferences with *Hangouts*.

INSTAGRAM, owned now by *Facebook*, is less viral than other platforms because people can share only when they double click on the 'heart', making it difficult to push people to your site. Its culture is more geared to a younger set, teens and young adults. Like many platforms, *Instagram* is a hashtag based medium which allows users to aggregate images around particular events and subjects. It's also not a great environment for selling. For metrics, there's *Statagram* to measure how you're doing.

TUMBLER tracks people's interests and is generally geared toward fashion, entertainment and all that's 'cool.' This is where cool teens hang out. That means no 'stock' photos and lots of short animated GIFs. Use Union metrics to measure success.

PINTEREST is a virtual pinboard, echoing what teens might have posted on the inside of their lockers in high school and allows small businesses to showcase their product offerings, while also developing their own brand's personality. *Pinterest* is more of an 'aspirational' platform, where people post what they want and 'aspire' to own. Here, you can link to your website, which makes it great for business. It is currently used mostly by women. Because it is image-driven, businesses should use only great photos. It's also very searchable, perfect for Google and businesses of all types.

TWITTER lets you broadcast your updates across the web. This is perhaps the most fertile ground of social media, the 'cocktail party' of the internet. Here, you get a lot more credit for listening than for talking, and the one place you can enter into a conversation without coming across as pushy. But your tweets need to be good – relevant and thoughtful–to break through the noise. Mix up your official-related tweets about specials, discounts, and news updates with some fun and quirky tweets. Be aware of the trending topics, answer people's questions when possible, and remember, this is a cocktail party, so don't brag – say 'thank you' when someone says something nice.

REDDIT, like *StumbleUpon* or *Digg*, is ideal for sharing compelling content. With over 2 billion page views a month, *Reddit* has incredible social media marketing potential, but marketers should be warned that only truly unique, interesting content will be welcomed. It's also GIF friendly.

LINKEDIN is a great venue for entering into a professional dialog with people in similar industries and provides a place to share content with like-minded individuals. Encourage customers or clients to give your business a recommendation on your *LinkedIn*.

YOUTUBE is the number one place for creating video content, which can be an incredibly powerful social attraction tool. Many businesses try to create video content with the aim of having their video "go viral," but in reality the chance of that happening is pretty slim. Instead, focus on creating useful, instructive "how-to" videos.

For brick and mortar businesses, social media platforms like *Yelp*, *FourSquare*, and *LevelUp* are great. Register on these sites to claim your location spot, and then consider extra incentives such as check-in rewards, coupons or special discounts. Remember, these visitors to the store will have their phones in hand so they will have access to providing reviews.

III. CONVERTING PROSPECTS AND CUSTOMERS

You've done everything right to attract a visitor to your site. Now what? Here, we come to the most important role of a website: getting people to **ACT**, converting a visitor to a prospect. A prospect is a person whose name and email address you know. A customer is someone who has completed a transaction, registration or other "completion" action which automatically provides their name and email address and can be used for future contact.

A. PROMPTS: THE CALL TO ACTION (CTA)

While the principal goal of marketing is to prompt action toward a transaction, this is rarely accomplished in one giant step. Marketing is actually a process of small steps (or actions) designed to reduce the resistance and increase the benefit of a transaction. At each step/action along the way to a transaction, the visitor or prospect needs to feel encouraged and that for each step, the benefit outweighs the risk or they are giving up an entitlement/benefit if they do not act.

And, there's a reason for this resistance.
It's called the Amygdala.

THE NEUROSCIENCE OF COMMITMENT

The Amygdala is part of our brain within our brain that has a mind of its own. And, unlike its neighbor the frontal lobe, it's not so logical. Derived from our early ancestor, the lizard, this reptilian part of our brain has an interesting peculiarity, built in as a survival response, far older than the frontal, "thinking" parts of our brain.

It makes snap judgments and doesn't like risk. For the Amygdala – commitment before experience – is a bit of conundrum. How are you supposed to *experience* something new without first committing to it?

We find the answer among the reptiles. You may have heard the story which some claim is actually true: that a frog placed in boiling water will jump out, but if it is placed in cold water that is slowly heated, it will not perceive the danger and flop around until eventually becoming a cooked frog.

The path from stranger to visitor, prospect and customer is a gradual progression from cold water to hot. What gets them into the water is the perception of low risk and high benefit. A small commitment, but a commitment nonetheless.

Apart from the Amygdala, the competing frontal lobe, also has a mind of its own. It, too, is conservative minded, only on the opposite side. The way the thinking part sees it, if you're already in the water, it must be OK. Frontal lobes are averse to switching once they've committed to something. Frontal lobes think, "I've made an investment and unless there's more serious risk, I'll keep at it." So you have these two forces: risk aversion and avoiding sunk cost that leads to the primary principle of marketing: Small Steps Lead to Big Commitments.

That's just how the brain works. And that's how we get conversions. The key to moving a visitor to a customer is by moving the visitor step by step from one small action to another so they become engaged with a process of increased commitment and reduced risk.

The nature of a conversion varies by business type. Online businesses want an online purchase; bricks and mortar businesses, want a visit, call or request for further information. If visitors do not make a purchase or request information, the next best conversion is to capture the contact information so you can eventually interact with them. Ultimately, you want the email address...through purchase, download or other action. Whatever it takes.

START HERE

Sign Up Now

Click Here for
More Info

Click Here
To Purchase Tickets

REGISTER

Register Now

Click here to join now!

Click here to register now

**CLICK HERE TO
BECOME A MEMBER**

Click Here Now!

download

Donate Now
CLICK HERE!

ONLINE
STORE
CLICK HERE

click here to
order online

ACTION STEPS

A "Call To Action" (CTA) is a prompt for visitors to take specific actions that lead to further engagement and qualification. the goal is to capture an email address whether through purchase, request for further contact, or through an offer which requires their email address. Not all CTAs need to be requests for purchase, contact or offer. CTAs take the form of action verbs such as: Call, Buy, Register, View, Subscribe, Donate, Request, Click, Contact, etc. and can/should be accompanied by 'words of urgency' such as:

- Offer **expires** (date)
- **Daily** Special
- Order **now** and receive a free gift

CTAs generally fall into three categories:

TRANSACTIONAL, where you create sufficient value that a visitor becomes a customer through purchase or download of a virtual or actual product service, such as:

- **Buy**
- **Purchase**
- **Download**
- **Donate**

CONTACTUAL, where a visitor is converted to a prospect

when you create sufficient value that a visitor is motivated to contact you directly or provide their email address and/or phone number, whether or not there is an immediate deliverable or purchase. Examples:

- **Call** now
- **Request** a brochure, quotation, etc.
- **Subscribe** (for newsletters, etc.)
- **Register** (for sweepstakes, events etc.)

INTERACTIONAL, where you prompt visitors to become more engaged through interaction with content on your site, but not necessarily to result in conversion to the status of either prospect or customer by virtue of requiring neither contact information nor transactions. Examples include:

- **Watch** This Video
- **Take** a Survey
- **View** Examples

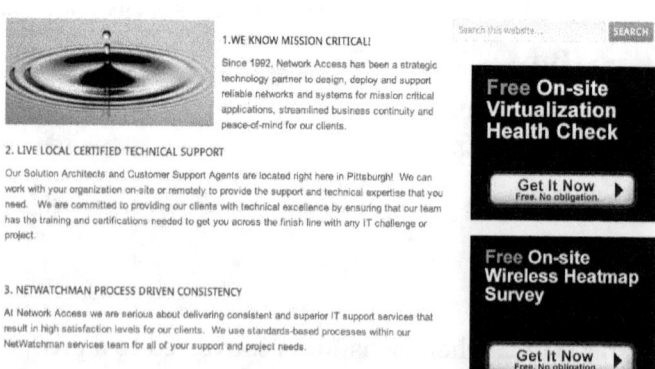

CLICK HERE! Getting People to ACT

As users, we may believe that the best websites are those that do not direct us along a particular path or outcome, but rather are path 'neutral.' While it is true that users need to feel that their actions are not being manipulated or limited, as the business owner you have an interest in prompting action toward commitment. Although you cannot control a visitors action path, it is possible to influence it through 'directive cues'. These provide a guide so the visitor can follow a particular sequence of steps toward action, based on their need. The steps may vary depending on the visitor's familiarity with the site. For example, a 'Newbie,' will be interested in different things than the returning visitor or 'regular.' In general, the fundamental elements of directed cues revolve around a few concepts, outlined in the next pages.

A STARTING POINT. What is the first thing a new visitor should do. If you leave it up to the visitor to just start exploring your site through your navigation bar, they may not get a clear idea of where to go. For example, a short video that provides an overview of what you do might be the easiest way for a visitor to become engaged with your company, product or service. The video can present two or three options for 'next step,' with an incentive/reason to proceed such as 'call,' 'download our ...' or other action. Here are some others:

- **Start your Search.** If you have a product search tool, call it out.
- **Landing Pages.** Particularly when linked from an ad or blog entry, visitors should be directed to a landing page relevant to the content where the link originated.
- **Download Free.** A CTA "offer."
- **Specials/Featured Items.** These are featured items that provide examples.

A 'STEP 2.' To the extent possible, on each page, there should be at least one prompt to action to make sure that if the visitor did not respond to the 'first step' prompt, there is a step 2 awaiting them. One form of prompt is a Sequence Chart that would explain your process as "3 Steps to ..."

INTERACTIONS.

In addition to specific steps, you can provide a variety of interactions that will prompt visitors to leave reviews, feedback, etc. Even if your site is a commerce site, these can be valuable. But for a content site, these interactions are an important part of creating user loyalty. Here are some suggestions:*

YOUR MAILING LIST. Adding a mailing list to your website allows you to reach out to customers and offer incentives to get them to return to your site in the future. Use a reputable email list management service like *MailChimp* to store your addresses and consider offering some type of incentive (like a free product or coupon code) to encourage sign-ups.

PRODUCT REVIEW FEATURES. Customers love to share their feedback, so make it easy for them to do so by adding product review features to your website's pages. Review modules can be custom-coded to your site or they can be easily installed using scripted programs like *Citricle* or *Re-Vu*.

SOCIAL SHARING TOOLS ON YOUR BLOG. Make it simple for website visitors to engage further with your site's content by embedding social sharing tools like *AddThis* or *ShareThis* into your site's blog posts and pages.

REQUEST COMMENTS ON BLOG POSTS. Want your site's visitors to leave comments on your blog posts? Simply ask them to do so! Ending your blog posts with a question and a prompt for readers to leave their thoughts in the comments section can be a great way to drive post based activity on your site.

"GAMIFICATION." Like badges, user contests and user profile rating systems – turn on-site activity into an engaging game. Tools like *Badgeville* and *BigDoor* make adding these elements simple, though larger companies may want to consult developers in order to create their own custom game-based activity reward systems.

USER ENGAGEMENT. Solicit user feedback on future product launches. As mentioned above, consumers love to provide input on their preferences and buying habits – so don't let this valuable source of market research data go to waste! If you're thinking about rolling out a new product or service offering, solicit feedback from potential customers on your website. Doing so will not only help ensure the success of your eventual launches, it'll go a long way towards driving on-site user activity by giving visitors the impression that their interests are taken seriously.

RECOMMEND "RELATED READING." Once readers have landed on your company's blog posts, don't lose them to the "Back" button. Instead, encourage them to stick around by adding extensions and plug-ins that automatically display related posts. Sharing recommended reading articles is a great way to keep visitors on your site and engaged with your content.

"Q&A." Don't just set up a static FAQ page – create a "Q&A" section that's expanded in response to user questions. Giving visitors a place to ask questions and continually updating the page with your responses makes for an engaging feature that's sure to lead to a boost in on-site activity rates.

VARY CONTENT FORMATS. Last – but not least – freshen up your content by formatting it in different ways, including text, image and video-based posts. Different readers respond to different types of content in different ways, so by including a number of different formats, you'll encourage user activity on your site by appealing to all of these various preferences.

*http://blog.hostgator.com/2013/04/09/11-ways-to-encourage-user-activity-on-your-site/

B. THE PRIZE (THE EMAIL ADDRESS)

Not all conversions are transactions. In the absence of a transaction, the next best thing is a conversion to a prospect, defined as the name and email address and any other information that will allow you to have ongoing contact.

If you have been successful in attracting a visitor to your site, a good deal of the expense of marketing has already been incurred. But, without an email address, you have lost the opportunity to continue to contact your prospect. To prompt a visitor to provide information, you need to have a no-cost, relevant and valuable offer. Some examples include:

REGISTRATIONS, including:
- **Contests**
- **Special offer** notifications
- **White papers**, newsletters, updates
- **Product** availability

DOWNLOADS, including:
- **Assessments**, surveys or audits
- **White Papers**, research or booklets
- **Price Sheets**, specifications
- **Trial Use**, if you have virtual products that allow for such use

IV. TRANSFORMING

Once you have converted a visitor to either a prospect or customer, you now have the most valuable tool in marketing: the email address. That allows you to continue the relationship by transforming first time prospects and customers into repeat customers, Clients of the Future (COFs) and advocates for your business, service and product.

A. THE POWER OF OUTBOUND MARKETING

Outbound marketing strategy is essential for any company that needs to nurture leads as a key marketing activity. There are very few companies that could successfully make the case for every new lead being a sales-ready lead. This is particularly true of B2B (business to business) buyers because they often do a lot of research and analysis prior to making a purchase decision, and the buying cycle can be weeks or months.

Outbound Marketing is also critical for companies that expand their footprint and revenue potential inside existing customers over time. Mining your accounts for new selling opportunities is something that can be executed far more efficiently with well-planned marketing campaigns that identify new revenue opportunities.

B. REPEAT VISITS

Whether or not someone has purchased from you, by agreeing to provide their email address, prospects have signaled that you have begun a relationship. Like all relationships, they need to be nurtured. At this point, there are two goals:

- Return/repeat visit to your website or business
- Referral/advocacy

A return visit to either your website or your bricks and mortar business can be prompted in a number of ways:

A BLOG. A blog lets you provide timely and updated content that is relevant to your site and its visitors. Adding a blog encourages people to return to your site in order to stay informed on up-to-date news.

CHAT ROOM. Chat rooms are real-time online conversations that typically take place in a predetermined internet medium like through a website or an online chat software program. Adding a chatroom to your website (especially at regular, predetermined intervals you set) encourages active communication and involvement that brings visitors back time and time again.

MESSAGE BOARD. A message board is an online forum where people hold discussions based on posts to one another. It differs from chatrooms because the exchange does not take place in "real-time", but it does provide consistent input from your site's visitors that keeps them coming back.

WIDGETS, GAMES, POLLS OR CONTESTS. Adding a widget, game, or poll that is relevant to the content of your site is a great way to keep visitors engaged while they're on your site, and to encourage them to return once they leave. If you mix in a contest within your poll, game, or widget, you ensure that people will remain interested and likely encourage them to come back to see if they've won.

SOCIAL NETWORKING BUTTONS. Almost everyone online is tapped into some social media network, and you should tap into that too by including social networking buttons for all of the major social networking tools (see the section on social media).

FREE STUFF. Give something away – a free e-book, screensaver, mobile application, widget, or music download that is relevant to the content of your site or your visitor's interests. Remember to make your giveaways relevant to your website so you don't end up with a hodge-podge of free junk thus causing your visitors to lose interest.

SPECIAL DEALS TO LOYAL VISITORS. Offer coupons, discounts, free shipping, or exclusive deals to loyal returning visitors. Use the enticement of special deals as a way to capture customer information (i.e. email addresses) to use in your email marketing campaign.

WEBINARS. Everyone wants to learn something new. Establish yourself as a thought-leader in your field by offering a monthly or quarterly webinar on an informative and educational topic. Consider trying *Dimdim* Webinars for free for 30 days to get started.

REPEAT REWARDS. There's a reason popular brands offer "VIP" clubs that grant repeat buyers access to special rewards and discounts. To build loyalty and drive both on-site activity and sales amongst your existing customers, consider implementing some type of visit that rewards visitors based on their purchase or engagement history. These systems can be as simple as creating a manual list of top buyers who receive special promotions or as complex as gamification-integrated programs that automatically profile and reward top users.

C. DRIP CAMPAIGNS

Drip campaigns are automated processes that send a set of messages or content to sales leads at the right moment to move them through the sales cycle. Drip campaigns allow you to consistently "touch" leads with relevant information based on time intervals, actions taken by prospects on your website, or other parameters, freeing up valuable marketing and sales resources without neglecting your prospects.

BENEFITS OF DRIP CAMPAIGNS

- **Timely.** The content is triggered by how a user is interacting with your brand and where they are in the sales cycle.
- **Effective.** Providing your sales team with a supply of leads that are ready to close, optimizing marketing and sales effectiveness.
- **Automated.** You spend less time pitching your product or service and more time closing deals.

TYPES OF CAMPAIGNS

- **Top of Mind**, help keep your leads engaged with your company, product or service throughout the process;
- **Educational**, providing relevant production information to prepare them for a purchase;
- **Re-engagement**, designed to win back the interest of colder leads;
- **Competitive**, target your competitor's customers with benefits of switching to your product;
- **Promotional**, entice prospects with limited time promotions and special pricing offers;
- **Training**, for new clients or use internally to move readers through a training program.

EXAMPLE: Drip campaigns can be employed to nurture prospects to a sales-ready state automatically, with no involvement from a marketing or sales team. Here's an example of a branching drip campaign:

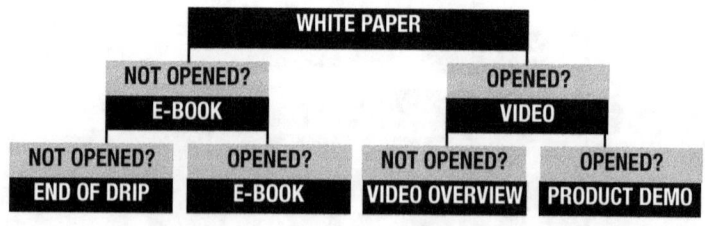

BEST PRACTICES

Target Your Campaign. Tailor your campaigns so that they target each segment of your prospect list with personal messages. The deeper your segmentation, the more personal your messages can be.

Design for Your Audience. Make it easy and painless for your prospects to express their preferences regarding frequency of messages, type of content they would like and how they would like to receive that content.

Test. Test your campaigns' effectiveness and continually evaluate which aspects are working best, review campaign goals and metrics like opens, click-throughs, and bounces.

Utilize Your Tools. Marketing automation tools also provide segmentation tools, social media connectors, analytics and CRM integration that make using drip marketing campaigns even easier.

*http://www.pardot.com/infographic/basics-drip-campaigns-infographic/

D. REFERRAL/ADVOCACY

Apart from getting visitors to return, is the role
these visitors play in introducing your site and/or
social media platforms to others. 92% of consumers
trust peer recommendations, where only 40% trust
search advertising; 36% trust sponsored ads on social
networking sites and 33% trust online banner ads.
And the average value of a referred customer is at
least 16% higher than that of a non-referred customer
with similar demographics and time of acquisition.
On average, referral recommendations result in 3 to
5 times higher conversion rates than other channels.
Interestingly, research has shown that recommending a
product or service to another person actually increases
that person's likelihood of buying, whether or not
they've previously purchased. There are several ways
you can create referral and advocacy from your visitors:

AN OFFER. Effective referral programs provide
customer advocates with a compelling reason to
share the program with their friends and encourage
friends to engage with the brand. Offering incentives
can dramatically increase, expand and encourage
participation. Successful offer structures share 4 key
components:

A COMPELLING OFFER FOR YOUR ADVOCATES. Give your customer advocates a reason to share with their friends. Successful offers are typically generous, unique, and targeted to a brand's customer base. Offers that give advocates an ongoing incentive to share such as internal offers (free goods, discounts, and loyalty points), gift cards, and charitable donations are ideal.

A UNIQUE OFFER FOR THE FRIEND. Motivate referred friends to try a brand's product or service. A unique offer that friends can't get anywhere else encourages potential new customers. Internal rewards, such as coupons for a percentage-off purchase or a free month subscription, are excellent friend offers.

A BALANCED OFFER STRUCTURE. Creating a balanced offer structure for customer advocates and their friends is critical. Maintaining a sense of equality and integrity gives advocates peace of mind and will motivate them to share.

TESTING AND OPTIMIZING. The final key to a successful offer structure is testing and optimizing to find what most effectively compels customers to become advocates for a brand. By trying different incentives and analyzing the data, marketers can find the optimal combination of customer advocate and friend rewards.

PROMOTING THE REFERRAL PROGRAM.

Driving awareness of a referral program is critical to its success. The more customers that see a referral program, the more they will become advocates and share the program with their friends. A best practice is for brands to promote their referral programs across channels, utilizing all of their available owned assets. The more customer advocates that are driven to the top of the referral funnel, the more friend conversions brands will see from their referral program, that can be accomplished in the following ways:

PROMOTIONAL PLACEMENTS ACROSS OWNED ASSETS.

A systematic approach to the promotion of referral programs, across all of a brand's owned assets, is an important factor in driving participation and directly relates to the success of the program. Brands should include promotions on their corporate websites (particularly the homepage), email promotions to their customers and opt-in lists, as well as on social networks.

PROMOTING AT KEY CUSTOMER TOUCH POINTS. Brands should promote the referral program in key touch points throughout the customer experience. Customers are most likely to share the program with their friends when they feel closest to the brand, typically after they have made a purchase or interacted with the product.

Promotions in key customer touch points such as order confirmation pages, purchase confirmation emails, pop-up messages and banner ads within digital products drive high-quality advocacy.

E. MAKING IT EASY FOR ADVOCATES TO REFER.

There are a number of ways in which advocates can share referral marketing programs with their friends, including email, personal URL (PURL), *Facebook*, *Twitter*, *Google+*, etc. Making sharing easy, and testing and optimizing messaging according to sharing channels are important components and directly related to the success of a referral program.

SELECTING SHARING CHANNELS FOR A REFERRAL PROGRAM. Depending on the type of business and offer, marketers should make different sharing channels available for advocates to share with their friends. Email is the most popular sharing channel in referral programs and should always be included. Consumer brands should also include *Facebook*, *Twitter*, and *Google+* for optimal results, and B2B companies should include *LinkedIn*, *Google+*, *Twitter* and/or *Facebook*. We recommend providing 2 to 4 sharing channels for advocates to choose from.

EMAIL SHARING. Email is the most popular sharing channel in a referral program because it's a personal share between an advocate and his or her friend. Since the email shares come as personal recommendations from a trusted source, the conversion rates are the highest of all sharing channels. Default messages for email sharing should read like a story with a personal touch, which tells the friend about the offer they will receive and what the advocate gets if the friend converts.

THE MESSAGE: DEFAULT VS. ADVOCATE CREATED.

A best practice is for brands to provide advocates with the options to use a default, pre-populated message or messages that they compose themselves. Personal messages (written by advocates) perform better than default messages created by the brand, but on average, 40% of advocates do not change the default share message.

PURL SHARING. PURLs are personalized links that brands can provide to advocates to share content with their friends across channels and platforms— emails, blogs, instant messages, social networks and more. Because PURLs are a simple, flexible sharing option that can be one-to-one (email) or one-to-many (*Facebook* posts), they are a very popular sharing

option. Since PURLs are links to be included in
multiple sharing channels, default messages do
not apply.

FACEBOOK/GOOGLE+ SHARING. Sharing via *Facebook*
and *Google+* is one-to-many sharing with an advocate's
friends and social communities. Shares to *Facebook*
and *Google+* see larger amplification than one-to-one
shares. Default messages for *Facebook* or *Google+*
sharing should sound like your advocates are speaking
directly to their friends and include the advocate's
rationale for why they are sharing the offer.

TWITTER SHARING. Sharing via *Twitter* is a one-to-
many, broadcast share. *Twitter* shares see the highest
amplification, or click-per-share rate because they
can be seen by anyone. Default messages for *Twitter*
should be more condensed for the world at large. It is
beneficial to use a @TwitterHandle and the name of
the brand within the post to increase SEO, as well as a
hashtag (#) attributed to the referral program.

PERSONALIZING THE FRIEND LANDING PAGE EXPERIENCE.

A simple and personalized friend experience fosters a high level of trust in the referral experience, which leads to engagement and conversion. One of the most effective ways to create a personalized experience is via the friend landing page. The friend landing page is the page that a friend sees upon clicking on a trusted recommendation from a customer advocate via email, *Facebook, Twitter, LinkedIn, Google+* or a PURL. The friend landing page should communicate what the referral program is about, communicate the offer and include a call to action (CTA) for conversion. A conversion can be an opt-in, sign up, redemption, or purchase. To optimize conversion, the friend landing page should follow these guidelines:

MAKE IT SHORT AND TO THE POINT. Keep the message concise and clear. Give the referred friend a quick overview of the offer and outline the steps to conversion.

MAKE IT PERSONAL. The best landing pages reinforce that the recommendation is from someone they trust. Ideally, the copy includes the name of the advocate who referred the friend.

DESCRIBE THE FRIEND-ONLY OFFER. Highlight the incentive, be clear about what the referred friend will receive and communicate that it is a "friends-only" deal. Friends need assurance that the reward they will receive is exactly what they were promised.

KEEP THE CTA SIMPLE. The CTA should be strong and concise. The friend landing page should provide a clear path to conversion in as few steps as possible.

V. CONCLUSION

Until a few years ago, entrepreneurs and business owners like George and Georgette would have had to worry only about local competition. They could personally engage customers, talk to them and get to know them. Although, in many cases, this is still true, the internet has enabled them to extend their reach beyond local boundaries, engaging people in new ways through the online promotion, social media and mobile interaction, creating more opportunity than ever before. But just as the opportunity for George and Georgette has expanded, so it is for other businesses like theirs across the country and the world.

And like all marketing, the primary goal of internet marketing is to get people to take action by attracting them to your website, blog or social media platform, converting them to take some action toward a transaction or other measurable goal, including providing their contact information such as email and transforming them into loyal customers and advocates for your business, product or service.

In the preceding pages, we've seen that whether your website provides principally communication, commerce, community or informative content (or a combination), the culture of the internet requires a more immediate, interactive, visual and narrative style to adapt to shorter attention spans and choice. And, it often takes a combination of traditional marketing methods such as media advertising, public relations and personal interaction in concert with online marketing, to attract, convert and transform customers.

In the case of attracting customers, we've seen that there are three basic "M" strategies, including:

Megaphone Marketing, where, through both traditional and online interuptive methods and models such as PPI, PPC and PPA methods and public relations you can promote your business and attract visitors.

Magnetic Marketing or SEO, where relevant content, markers, backlinks and syndication leverages search engines to allow people to find you.

Meetups or Social Networks that leverage the context and culture of the internet and utilize a variety of social networking platforms to engage people and create communities of interested prospects and customers.

In the case of conversion, once people have found you and visited your site, we've seen the importance of the underlying motivations of visitors, based on the latest neuroscience research and through specific methods, how to prompt action through offers and other incentives to lower resistance and increase the benefit of action. Even when a purchase is not the outcome, an important goal is to prompt visitors to provide the ultimate prize, their contact information, especially their email address, so that they can be reached in the future.

Having the email address allows businesses to begin the transformation process through ongoing outbound marketing, drip campaigns and interaction that can prompt repeat visits, referral and advocacy for your business, product or service. It is through this transformation from visitor, prospect, customer and advocate that we can personalize the experience and create stronger bonds with our customers.

Many businesses choose to operate exclusively online, providing great flexibility in monetizing traffic. The appendix outlines the nine principal ways that traffic can be monetized to build successful online businesses.

Whether you have a bricks and mortar, online or combined business, using some or many of these methods can help you attract, convert and transform your customers to help your business grow. Best of luck in creating ACTion for your business.

VI. APPENDIX: ONLINE BUSINESS MODELS

Although there are many ways that websites can help promote a bricks and mortar business, more and more companies are turning to online business opportunities. Here are some strategies to monetize the traffic on your site.

A. ADVERTISING

As previously noted, Pay Per Click (PPC) advertising generates revenue whenever someone clicks on an ad on your website, while Pay Per View (PPV) pays based on the number of views (or impressions). Both rely heavily on traffic volume and targeted content, and although this may seem like an easy way to make money, don't expect to retire anytime soon unless you have a huge site with lots of highly targeted articles. *Google AdSense* is one of the most widely used Pay Per Click engines.

B. SPONSORSHIP / PRIVATE AD SALES

Similar to the Pay Per View model, this monetization strategy usually involves you going directly to the advertiser instead of dealing with an ad network. This form of advertising model usually involves you doing the leg work to approach potential advertisers. Before you do, make sure your website content is highly targeted and generating a lot of traffic.

C. PHYSICAL PRODUCTS

This is the age-old model of selling actual physical products. Many large online retailers use this model successfully – for example, *Amazon* or *Dell*. Selling physical products involves listing one or multiple products for sale on your website, facilitating a secure transaction and shipping the product. Keep in mind there are warehousing and distribution elements to this model unless you use drop shipping (and shipping to overseas destinations can be cost prohibitive).

D. DROP SHIPPING

Drop shipping is similar to the physical product model, but with someone else looking after the warehousing and distribution. You establish a relationship with one or more businesses who look after the physical goods you're selling – you only have to worry about sales. When a customer purchases a product on your website, you oversee the transaction, then forward the order through to your drop shipper who packages and distributes the goods.

E. DIGITAL PRODUCTS

Digital products are anything you can download –
ebooks, software, music, videos. Digital products
are relatively easy, as they have a much lower cost of
sale than physical products. With a digital product
there's no physical warehousing, shipping or cost to
manufacture the product. You can create your own
products to sell, pay someone to develop a product for
you, or promote other people's products via affiliate
networks (see the affiliate products section below).

F. AFFILIATE PRODUCTS

Many website owners make money from promoting
other people's products and services. To start
promoting, you apply to become affiliated with a
merchant, either via one of the many affiliate networks
or directly. When you refer a customer to the merchant,
you receive a commission on sales. There are affiliate
networks for both physical and digital products as well
as for lead generation, otherwise know as Cost Per
Action (CPA) offers. For physical products *Amazon* has
its own network, while *Clickbank* is one of the larger
digital product networks.

G. MEMBERSHIP / SUBSCRIPTION

Membership sites make money by charging people a regular fee to have access to a secure "Members Only" area. This area might contain training material that's updated or added to regularly, or it might be a web-based application. If you want customers to stick around and keep paying for the privilege then you need to make sure you provide unique and quality content.

H. MARKETPLACE

Marketplaces are dating sites, freelance marketplaces such as *99designs* and auction sites like *eBay*. Usually marketplaces make money by charging sellers a fee to list items for sale, or from advertising if the site generates enough traffic. One of the biggest challenges with marketplace sites is attracting enough buyers and sellers to interact regularly.

I. SERVICES

The services model encompasses a huge variety of offerings and usually involves customers paying for someone's time. Selling a service may involve selling day to day tasks such as data entry or professional services such as accounting. Services can prove hard to scale, as usually you need to keep adding work-hours as your clientele grows.

ABOUT THE AUTHOR

Dan Droz, designer, entrepreneur and educator is president of Droz and Associates, a leading brand and marketing consultancy in Pittsburgh, PA and for 18 years, served as Adjunct Professor of Design Management at Carnegie Mellon University, where he directed the Design for Business Project and co-founded the first university-based Interdisciplinary Product Development and Innovation program in the nation. He has been recognized 15 times as a "Marketer of the Year" by the American Marketing Association, including "Grand Marketer of the Year" in 2012, and one of 6 Distinguished Design Alumni at the 25th Anniversary of Carpenter Center for the Visual Arts at Harvard University, his alma mater. Droz and Associates is a multi-disciplinary marketing team that helps organizations create trust, engagement and commitment with their audiences with differentiated marketing plans, brands and online and traditional marketing programs.